I0567397

How to Learn Anything

Advanced Learning Strategies for Unlimited Memory

(Learning Through the Brain's Fastest Superlinks Learning Style)

Stanley Smith

Published By **Bella Frost**

Stanley Smith

*How to Learn Anything: Advanced Learning
Strategies for Unlimited Memory (Learning
Through the Brain's Fastest Superlinks Learning
Style)*

ISBN   978-1-998769-32-2

No part of this guidebook shall be reproduced in any form without permission in writing from the publisher except in the case of brief quotations embodied in critical articles or reviews.

Legal & Disclaimer

The information contained in this ebook is not designed to replace or take the place of any form of medicine or professional medical advice. The information in this ebook has been provided for educational & entertainment purposes only.

The information contained in this book has been compiled from sources deemed reliable, and it is accurate to the best of the Author's knowledge; however, the Author cannot guarantee its accuracy and validity and cannot be held liable for any errors or omissions. Changes are periodically made to this book. You must consult your doctor or get professional medical advice before using any of the suggested remedies, techniques, or information in this book.

Upon using the information contained in this book, you agree to hold harmless the Author from and against any damages, costs, and expenses, including any legal fees potentially resulting from the application of any of the information provided by this guide. This disclaimer applies to any damages or injury caused by the use and application, whether directly or indirectly, of any advice or information presented, whether for breach of contract, tort, negligence, personal injury, criminal intent, or under any other cause of action.

You agree to accept all risks of using the information presented inside this book. You need to consult a professional medical practitioner in order to ensure you are both able and healthy enough to participate in this program.

Table Of Contents

Chapter 1: Improving Your Memory 1

Chapter 2: Reading For Learning 11

Chapter 3: The Art Of Summary 22

Chapter 4: Timing 26

Chapter 5: Using Mnemonics 30

Chapter 6: The Feynman Technique 33

Chapter 1: Improving Your Memory

An excellent memory is key to any learning endeavor. Without it, all your efforts to learn will be futile. It's not worth learning if you can't remember what you just learned.

It is worth noting that you will need to have sufficient memory. Although a sufficient memory can be achieved, perfection is reserved for a select few. Remember that you can achieve a good memory. Your efforts should be focused on yourself and not other people. Comparing yourself with other people will only make you miserable. Be the only person you want to beat every single day. There is no one else.

You need to practice patience and develop a strong memory. It's not something you can do in a few hours. It takes hard work but the best thing about consistency, it breeds excellence, including in the area of memory.

Mind Exercise

Your brain should be treated like a muscle. If you do, strength gains will follow. Although the brain isn't physically strong, it can be developed in much the same way as your leg or chest muscles. The brain is similar to a muscle. It also has muscle memory. This memory allows the brain to perform certain movements correctly, such as shooting basketballs or kicking footballs.

A condition called atrophy, where a muscle's strength and mass shrinks, can be caused by a failure to exercise or use it consistently. Although your brain won't actually shrink, it could affect your mental performance, strength, or abilities. Therefore, it is crucial to train your mind frequently and intensely.

Your memory goes hand in hand what goes with your mind. Your memory can be improved by keeping your mind engaged.

How does one train the mind to have a good memory? There are many ways to do it, but these are the main principles.

1. New Material

Diversity is an important contributor to your brain's ability to be flexible and adaptive over time. An inability to learn something new can cause mental stagnation, reduced cognitive performance, and worsened memory. To keep your brain flexible and alert, you must be exposed to new and unfamiliar information. The brain learns more as it is used to regular exercise.

2. Mental Challenges

Your mind will be most productive when you have to focus. Your mental exercises and activities will not be complete if you aren't challenged enough. It must force you to think more clearly than you usually do. You might learn a new language, or play a different musical instrument. These types of tasks require the involvement of multiple segments of the brain. The limbic, which controls your memory, is found deep in the temporal brain. Memory capacity can be increased through constant activation.

3. Baby Steps

To help you improve your memory, the best exercises are those that take each step one at a time rather than doing it in one big leap. You will learn more if you take small steps and not all at once. It is easier to learn a step or topic one at a while, which will give you the opportunity to win many smaller victories over time that can build your foundations for success. This approach can also give your brain a sense accomplishment each time you move a step closer to understanding the next principle.

4. Fulfillment:

If you feel fulfilled or rewarded by the mental or brain exercises you do, you will likely continue to do them until they bear fruit. Your risk of failing to benefit from the results and dropping out increases. This is why taking huge steps to improve your memory and learn new skills are not always the best way. You would be more successful if you were patient and worked your way up.

In the next chapters, you will learn many of these exercises which not only enhance your memory but also help you to master virtually any task with a higher level of dexterity.

Let's get Physical

Your cognitive and mental performance can be significantly improved by exercising your mind. For those who want to make a real difference in your memory development, you should consider including physical exercises. Exercise has been shown to increase blood circulation and oxygen delivery to brains, which can help improve mental sharpness.

Regular exercise helps reduce stress hormones, and increases the beneficial effects of brain chemicals like endorphins. The brain secretes chemicals that can cause a positive experience similar to morphine. These chemicals also work as natural painkillers. Exercising regularly helps maintain neuroplasticity and creates growth factors.

Aerobic exercise is crucial for physical exertion. Aerobic exercises can help improve blood flow to your brain, making it a stronger, more efficient pump. It is believed that exercises that increase heart strength and health are very helpful in promoting brain performance.

It is important to exercise at a time that is convenient for you. Morning exercise is the best when it comes to timing. For those who want to develop a good memory, getting started in the morning is key. You might find yourself struggling to get up in the morning if you don't run.

Morning exercises not only help with memory development, but they can also improve mood and decrease the chance of having a bad afternoon. Increased blood circulation is the true reason aerobic exercises can help you improve mental performance and your memory. When it comes to such exercises, you don't need to train at the gym during lunch. To maximize your mental performance for the future, simply walk for 20 minutes around the block or to the mall next to your office.

Sleeping is good for your memory

Do not misunderstand that I love coffee. I especially love strong brews. I find it helps me through particularly slow days and when I am busy, during the night. Despite my deep love for coffee, and its ability to keep you awake and alert, I realized that not even a cup of it can make you feel as alert and awake throughout the day. I feel more awake when I sleep well at night and can get the work done without the need for coffee. It's only that I get that extra edge from coffee, even though it's not my foundation for great mental performance.

For most people 8 hours seems to be the required time. This isn't always the case. This is a great way to gauge your sleeping habits, but it's quite possible that you will need more sleep than 8 hours every night.

How do you find out how much you need to get the best cognitive abilities? This can be done by writing down your sleep history for the next 2 weeks. Note in your journal the time you fell asleep at night and the time when you woke you up the next morning. Keep track of how sleepy you felt that night, the hours you slept, and the mood you had throughout the day. Be especially aware of days where you were tired or sluggish. Within two weeks, your minimum sleep requirement will be known.

You might consider these options if quality sleep is a problem at night.

* A regular sleeping routine: It's important to sleep and wake up at the same times each night and every day to ensure quality sleep. Habits are the foundation of all life on Earth, including humans. Consistency in your sleep will benefit your body and mind. Do your best to go to bed at the same time each night, wake up at the

identical time every morning, even on weekends!

Turn off your screens. The main reason you can't get a good nights sleep is the light emitted from all electronic screens (computer screens, TV screens) and television screens. The light from these screens can cause you to have trouble sleeping at night. It suppresses the body's ability release melatonin. In addition, white light triggers the body's wakeup mechanisms, which can result in much-regretted insomnia. To be mentally sharp, you need to stop checking your electronics for at least 30 mins before bed.

* Give up the Caffeine. Many people struggle to sleep with caffeine. There's a good chance you could be one of them. You should quit drinking your late afternoon coffee for deep, restful sleep.

Chapter 2: Reading for Learning

You need to be able read well to have a great memory. Reading is the best way to learn.

While it may seem simple to read to learn, it is far from easy. Many people may think reading to learn is too simple. This could be why it can be difficult for them to master new skills. There are reading strategies that can make it easier to learn new things. And one of those techniques is the SQR3, which stands for survey, question, and reading-recitation-reviewing. This reading technique can help you recall more of what you've read by repeatedly approaching the reading materials with similar approaches.

Repetition is key to being able remember or recall information. Engaging with a topic more often will result in a deeper integration of the information into our long-term mental memories. Many students will go through their materials at least three or more times before they feel comfortable with them. This is also why it is almost impossible to study before an exam.

This should be more than just repetition. It should also be systematic and methodical. Not just a repetitive loop. The SQR3 technique is here to help. Let's examine each component of this technique in more detail.

The Survey

This is a summary or general overview of your material. This process is intended to give you a general idea of what the text is talking about. This is often called scanning.

This step assumes that your mind prefers to view the whole picture first before seeing the individual parts. This will help you understand what you are reading and the general tone of the discussion.

If you have a general idea about the arrangement or logical order of the material's flow you can create a mental structure or framework that will help you to better understand the materials.

If, for instance, you are looking at a piece of learning material and notice the author reasoning in cause-and effects, it is easy to pick up the material by anticipating a discussion about a cause, or several causes, and the resulting effects.

How can you survey your books effectively? Here are some great surveying methods that you can use for books.

* You should always read blurbs if the book or material that you are reading has them. Blurbs can be short reviews or testimonials of the material. They are often included on a book's dust jacket or

back cover. This is a great introduction to the content that follows.

* Read the book's table-of-contents to get an idea about what topics will be covered and how they are organized.

* Read the chapter overviews, objectives, and outline pages if they are included in the book.

* Refer to the beginning chapter's headings (major and sub) for discussion questions, if any.

These surveying tips are also useful for other materials like articles and modules.

* Look through the materials if they have an overview or abstract.

* Look for major and sub headings.

* Make sure to read any summary or conclusion that is included at the end. This

may sound strange at first, but it will prepare your brain for what's to come.

Ask and You Shall Receive...(Questions)

Reading can be made a fun and engaging way to learn. You can ask questions about the materials that you have read. These questions may be based upon the images, graphics, headings, or chapters in your reading material.

Imagine that you're reading a Ketogenic Diet article as a method to lose weight. Some of the questions you might ask yourself before reading an article on the Ketogenic Diet could be:

What does the Ketogenic diet do to help you lose body fat?

What are the most important features of the Ketogenic Digestion and what sets it apart from other diets.

How can I minimize the negative health effects of diet and what are my options to reduce them?

These questions can be asked after reviewing your learning materials. This will allow you to concentrate more on what's being read. Your mind will actively seek out the answers so you can retain the information better.

Read (R1)

Now it's the time to go to the meat. You should not just sift through the information. Note or highlight any important or critical points in the book. Better yet, go back and read the highlighted points to make sure you understand them.

If your learning materials are printed, don't be shy about making notes in the margins. These important notes could be similar or opposed examples, cross references, agreements or summaries. Research has shown that the brain retains only 10% of what it reads. This means that taking notes to help remind you of what was read can dramatically improve your ability to learn. It is also a good idea to create diagrams or tables of the learning materials. This will allow you to represent the ideas visually and make it easier to comprehend.

Do not worry if you do not have electronic copies of your learning material. Just make notes and draw diagrams on a separate piece of paper or notebook to highlight the main points and ideas that you come across in the material. You can refer to these pages later by making sure you indicate the page number. You can then go back to your earlier questions after the survey has ended and answer them.

Recitation (R2)

Recitation is second among the 3 R's. Through various methods, such as explaining and reciting key ideas and concepts to someone else, recapping them out loud, paraphrasing, or summarizing the material by main point or chapter, you will be reproducing these key ideas.

Why is recitation important for reading and learning? Because it makes it possible to interact with your reading materials via echoing (remember, the importance repetition). To learn key concepts and points effectively, your auditory and visual senses must be activated.

Reviewing (R3)

The final piece of SQR3 technology caps your reading-learning experiences in ways that reinforce or deepen the lessons you have learned from new information. To review your learning materials:

* Take a look at the pages of the learning material. Read the headings and highlighted points.

* Review any summaries or abstracts you may have created about the learning materials. Make sure that they are in accordance with your learning materials' main ideas and points.

* Please read all questions and answers once more.

* Finally, make it seem like you will be giving a lecture on the learning material in front a lot of people. You can make this a casual summary or commentary about the material. Your knowledge of the topic must be clear and well-understood. You can make teaching look like studying. Give it a go.

Maximizing Reading-Learning Experience

In order to get the most out of your learning materials, you can do any or all these activities:

Write a poem, haiku, song or song about the subject of your learning material. Use the main ideas and points in the material to create words or lyrics for this literary masterpiece.

For Mac users, create a PowerPoint or KeyNote presentation about the learning materials you just finished reading.

Use diagrams, pictures, or charts to illustrate the key points, ideas, and concepts of the material. Your brain thinks in pictures. By doing this, you can simplify the concepts that you've learned and make them more understandable.

While it might seem like a lot, learning information and knowledge requires patience. However, this is not the end of the world. Do not be discouraged.

Although the first few steps of incorporating these techniques may seem tedious, it will become much easier over time. It will also help you retain the knowledge more quickly than just reading it over and over without making significant improvements.

Chapter 3: The Art of Summary

Paraphrasing requires only changing a few sentences to express the same message or idea. Summarizing should not be confused. Summarizing can be described as the process of simplifying or abbreviating an information resource into a smaller number of words, sentences, or phrases. Summarizing may be used to express the main ideas within a 10-page learning materials in just one or two paragraphs. Or, it can be used for expressing the main points or ideas of a section or paragraph in just one or two sentences. This gives you a lot more freedom to choose how you want to concentrate on your learning materials, according to your goals or needs. It removes the extraneous material and allows you to concentrate on the essential information.

Summarizing is an excellent way to learn anything.

* Spend time with condensing materials you like.

* Carefully consider the learning material you choose to condense. It requires you to be able to differentiate between important points or ideas and those that don't.

* Write the main ideas and points of the content in your own words. This allows the information to be understood and absorbed better by you.

* Learn how you can think critically and analyze better.

* Take note of the main points and ideas within your learning materials.

Summarizing: The Art of Mastery

There are three steps to this: retain key ideas and points, discard unimportant ones, as well as abbreviating your learning materials by removing details and narratives that are not necessary.

The purpose of summarizing learning material will vary depending on its content (e.g. mental exercise, reference material in future, information abstract or study book) and the information available. Some summaries reduce original learning materials' lengths to only 30%. Others can be as short as 5%!

For summarizing learning materials, a general rule is that the greater the informational value of the material, it should be condensed. It's because keeping the same condensation rates between a brief reading material and one that is more detailed will result in a longer summary for a dense learning material.

For example, let's take two learning materials. One is a 5-pager while the other is a 100 pager. The 5-page learning materials will have a summary rate of 20%. This means that you only need to write one page for the summary. However, for the 100-pager, you will have to write an 20-page summary. Which is hardly a summary! It is important to keep summarizing as short as possible, and only consider the ideas that are really important. Simplicity is key here.

It is important to ask good questions in order to be able summarize well. These questions include among others:

What's the purpose of summarizing this material, anyway?

What are the main ideas or points of this learning materials?

What is the one thing you find most important about this learning material.

What ideas or points cannot I leave out of the summary?

Chapter 4: Timing

Sometimes we think that learning strategies and techniques are simple. We just need to put more effort into learning more stuff. This is far from the truth. Learning is more than just effort. It's about timing. So, work hard and work smart. It is possible to learn more by knowing when the best time is to study or learn new things.

You need to identify the factors that make you feel alert and focused when studying or learning. These might include the following:

When do you feel the most alert, focussed, awake, and capable of concentrating - morning, afternoon, or night?

You need to know how long it takes you to focus on one subject or learning material.

What habits or techniques help you focus and concentrate mentally at peak levels?

The more you become aware of these things and when you are most productive and focused, the easier it is to plan out a schedule that will allow you to learn everything you want. To ensure maximum comprehension and retention, you must be able to cycle and time your learning activities.

Practical Tips to Cycling or Timing your Learning Activities

For maximum retention and comprehension of any subject, it is a good idea to study the most difficult topics at peak learning times. You can schedule learning activities for topics that are less complicated or difficult than at other times.

I, for instance, struggle to understand technical topics like programming or statistics. It's all downhill from 1 p.m. onwards. From around 1 p.m. to noon, I plan my computer programming/statistics studies. This helps me to better understand the topics. I wouldn't waste my time studying such topics late at night, when my motivation and energy are low and my interest is even less.

Pomodoro can be used to time or cycle your learning activities.

Pomodoro works in 30 minute cycles. You work for 25 mins, study for 5, and then take a rest for 5. This is regardless of whether you feel tired or are able to go on. Each fourth cycle, you increase the rest period by 5 minutes to 10. You should take regular, "forced", breaks after you have worked for 25 minutes. This is to keep your mind sharp and prevent fatigue. It is a long-distance mentality.

Prior to learning the Pomodoro strategy, my friend, a CEO at a national consultancy firm, was only able to stay productive for 5 hours each day. My friend, who is a CEO at a national consulting firm, was only able to work for 5 hours per day. He started to report that the Pomodoro technique allowed him to work 7 hours more. To maximize your learning activities, I highly recommend the Pomodoro Technique. After 25 minutes of studying, take a 5-minute rest (10 every fourth cycle). It doesn't really matter if you feel tired. Your mind will appreciate it and will reward you with extended learning sessions.

Chapter 5: Using Mnemonics

A mnemonic is an instrument that helps people remember information, such as passwords or lists of items. Mnemonics can be used as a learning or studying technique. They use almost anything that can aid in remembering or recalling information. Mnemonics can help you do this by assigning images to certain pieces of information.

To give you an idea, let's do a fun activity. This will help you to see how effective mnemonics are for learning. The objective is to recite the alphabet in reverse order, from Z-A. This means that the alphabet must be recited in reverse order. You might find this a bit overwhelming. If you don't, you're likely a genius.

Here are some mnemonics that can be used to memorize and recite backwards the alphabet and other words.

Chunking

This is the process of breaking down letters and numbers into manageable, easier-to-remember pieces of 3 to 4. It's similar to trying to eat a large portion of your favorite steak. The best way to enjoy it is to chop it into small pieces. To make it easier to remember, you can cut it into bite-sized pieces for our reverse alphabet example: ZYXW VIUTS RQP LKJ IHG FED CBA

Is this a familiar pattern? This is the same way that banks use to make it easy to remember your credit card numbers.

Make It Graphic

Have you ever wondered why the phrase "a picture is worth a thousand pictures"? The simple answer is that our minds are wired to think visually. This is why visual presentations are easier to recall than written or audio presentations. To use the reverse-alphabet example above, it is important to associate each letter with a graphic. It will make it easier for you to remember the letters. Make your pictures as crazy as possible. They will make them stand out more in your mind, and make it easier for you to remember them. The same principle applies to remembering other things.

Remembering codes or passwords is one of the most powerful uses of mnemonics. Let's see some examples of passwords and codes, and how mnemonics could help us remember them.

ihavbn - I Have A Very Big Neck

pmnia = Picking Our Nose Is Awesome

Chapter 6: The Feynman Technique

Richard Feynman, Nobel Peace Prize-winning scientist and physicist created this highly popular learning strategy to improve his ability to understand concepts quickly and efficiently. His highly acclaimed learning method can be validated only by the fact he's more than just a physicist.

The three key principles or steps of the technique are: teaching a child to review, organizing and summarizing. Transmission is an optional principle. However, it's highly recommended. Let's have a closer look at each.

Teaching a Child

You don't have to wait for your child to teach you the thing you want, although that would be great. This allows you to quickly and easily get to the core of the topic. It's a common assumption that if you cannot explain the material to an eight-year-old, you don't really get it.

Write the topic or subject you would like to learn on a blank page. Below that, you should write all you know about that topic/subject as if it were something you had to teach a child. This will help to simplify the topic, making it easier to comprehend and make the topic more accessible. It is important to remember that simplicity wins the race!

The act of writing down your ideas throughout the day in a language that's easy for an 8 year old child to understand helps you to fully understand a topic. You may find yourself struggling with particular areas while writing these ideas. This is simply because you don't have enough knowledge to explain the concepts in simple terms. Consider this an excellent opportunity for you to grow and expand your knowledge rather than seeing it as a setback.

Review

As I mentioned before, sometimes you might have knowledge gaps when studying or learning a topic. There are many reasons why you might struggle to connect important concepts or principles.

These are great opportunities to increase your knowledge and understanding of a particular topic. These are indicators that you have reached an important level in your understanding and learning of the topic. You're right! True competence is the ability to identify your learning abilities' limits and then work to expand them. This is where learning truly begins.

Once you identify your sticking issues for a specific topic or subject, it will give you a point of reference to go back and revise your learning material until you are able explain the sticking points in an easy-to-understand way to your child. You can concentrate more on areas where you have sticking points by going over the material again.

Organization and simplification

Once you've completed writing your notes so that an eight-year-old kid understands the topic or content of your learning materials, it is time to organize your notes so that the main points and ideas flow naturally and logically. Also, you should avoid technical jargon (emphasis placed on simplification) in your learning material. The point of this technique to teach the subject at the simplest level is not to include it.

Once you have finished simplifying the language and organizing it, start to read it aloud. Listen carefully to any confusing words. These are great signs that you still have to learn or understand certain aspects of the material.

Transmission

This optional last step or principle can be quite entertaining. This is the place where you actually communicate your learning material's key points to a child or another person who doesn't know much about it. This is the most important part of your application. If the child or person can clearly understand what I'm saying, that means they have successfully learned the topic enough to explain it in simple terms. If all you see is confusion and dazed eyes, then you might need to go back to the books.

Why is it important to learn?

Being able to learn new things makes it possible for us to have a fulfilling and happy life. It's impossible to continue living with only the skills and knowledge we had years ago. Everything around us is constantly changing. However, it's up to us to either adapt and keep pace or lose our way.

Some people think that learning is only possible through school or seminar attendance, or reading a book or article on a particular skill or subject. Although these are great examples of learning, there is much more to it.

Imagine how you developed as a child, a teenager, a young adult, and finally, if you are lucky, into your retirement years. There were many skills and new knowledge that we needed to acquire during this time.

We were taught how to walk, drive and how to interact with others. This knowledge was in addition to the knowledge we gained at school. We learned new technologies and new ways to accomplish old tasks.

As we age, our abilities to perform tasks are changed as we need to compensate to our reduced strength and agility. We develop creativity and make better use our skills and abilities. Also, we learn how to adapt and change with the world around.

Our life experiences have taught us how to solve problems, how to deal with situations differently, and how to make the most of them. IN SHORT, THERE IS NO END TO OUR CAPACITY FOR LEARNING NEW THINGS OR ADAPTING TO THE WORLD AROUND US.

Our brains do not get "full" like a hard drive or notebook. There is always more knowledge available and more learning. It behaves in this way because we need more knowledge and learning to stay on top.

Imagine if the DOS-based computers of today were still available. Imagine if you still used a word processor to create documents. Imagine how difficult life would be if our doctors didn't have access to the most recent treatments and testing.

Even with all this new technology, new knowledge, it wouldn't matter if we didn't learn it, make use of it, and take advantage. There is no reason to feel proud of your skills being outdated by three decades. It is okay to like things the same way they were, but it is vital that you keep up-to-date your skills.

If you're learning more from everyone around you than you, then you're in essence backwards. It is as if everyone stands in a straight line, then everyone moves ahead. You are still behind the rest, even though you haven't moved one inch.

It is possible to move forward with knowledge and learning. It can help you increase your knowledge, skills, and perceived value to other people. Even though knowledge doesn't make you better, it makes you more valuable. It makes you more attractive.

Importantly, we don't need to go back to school in order to learn. The only thing we need is to be open to new ideas and skills as they become available.

Curiosity can be a wonderful thing. To be curious about life, we should all strive to understand it better. It is not always the brightest or smartest who are the most successful people in the world. People who are able to see a problem and solve it, or identify a weak point and make it better, are the most successful.

One person is not able to do everything. It is important to first recognize what you can improve upon and then to seek the knowledge necessary to make that improvement. As a major league pitcher works hard to hit a curveball with his bat, so too must you work hard to make any weakness your strength.

Always remain curious, and look for new ways to learn and grow. Always try to find ways to improve things and to learn more. This is how knowledge is gained and success is achieved.

Why Would You Like to Learn?

Each person wants to know something. These reasons can vary depending upon what we are trying to learn but most fall under one of the following categories. Either we want to improve our skill or adapt to the world around us. A dream or desire might be fulfilled.

Courses can help us fulfill our dreams and goals to become doctors or lawyers. You might consider taking a class in a program that will make your life easier or increase your value in the workplace. Maybe we have something that makes a particular task more enjoyable and easy. No matter the reason, it's important to understand them.

Perhaps you aren't convinced that we really need a reason in order to do something or learn something. You might be technically correct. But it is important for us to recognize that we may not have the motivation to learn something if there is no reason. This means that you shouldn't waste your time and effort trying to learn something without a reason.

There are reasons we need to do the things you do. Our brains need reasons to devote resources to a certain effort or task. These reasons are crucial to our ability to stay focused on what we're doing. People who are interested in learning something do better than others who have to do it the same way.

If you are looking for a new skill and don't see the benefit, you might give up on it. Because your brain doesn't see the value in doing that task. You won't put in the effort. Instead, you will seek out any excuse to stop the progress and not try to apply yourself.

Your brain will be motivated to do better if it understands that learning the new skill will make you more secure and easier. You'll see the rewards of achieving your goal or learning the skills.

A baseball player must practice hard and be able to learn as much as possible in order to perform at a higher level, earn more money, and play longer. An office manager will seek to master the latest software and management methods to increase their value. They want to perform at a better level and earn more money.

It could be that you are looking for a way to improve your skills. You may want to improve your nutrition and fitness so you can run a faster distance. Or maybe you want to lose weight but need to learn more to get better results.

Whatever your reason for wanting or needing to learn something, it's important to know the reasons and what benefits you stand to gain from the new knowledge or skill. Understanding these concepts will allow you to stay motivated and put your best foot forward in the learning process.

You will get the most value from learning something if you ask yourself why. Write down the benefits of the new skill or information and consider the impact on your life. This new knowledge can make your life better. It could make your life easier. Will it make your life easier?

No matter how many benefits your new knowledge may bring, it is vital that you understand and recognize them. Because you don't know how much you could make, you need to be willing to work hard and give your best effort in order for the learning process to succeed. It is all about the rewards and benefits of dedication when it comes time to apply resources.

How can we learn?

It is important to understand how we learn. Although we often believe learning happens in a classroom, it isn't the case. We can learn from all aspects of our lives. Also, it doesn't take a professor to learn anything.

All of our senses help us learn. All of our senses. We use our eyes and ears to see and understand, our ears and senses of touch to feel and to hear. Our noses capture the scents around us, and sometimes our taste buds.

Learning by experience is one of most effective methods of learning. This includes what our senses are telling us about those experiences. Our senses provided us with feedback as we learned to walk, talk and communicate. We felt pain after we took that first step. We understood that we had to do something different and learn how balance works.

When we were learning how to cook, we relied on our senses to tell if something was good or not. Our senses of taste and smell helped us determine whether something was overcooked or had burned. Our senses were able to tell when something was in the oven too long and had burned.

The oven and open flames were taught to us by our senses of touch. When we touched a hot pot or pan, we felt pain. When assembling something, we even learned how tight to tighten a bolt and nut by using our senses of touch. You can read about them, but nothing beats experiencing them in action and using all of your senses.

It is possible to learn with more than one sense. This will improve the quality of the information you are able to absorb and the time it takes to retain it. To learn, we must not rely solely on our ears and eyes. This might work for some people, but it may not be the best way to learn. However, this does not mean that these people are less intelligent and unable to learn. It simply means that they must learn differently to other people.

Every experience we have has an input. Each response is saved somewhere in our brain. It is now stored in different parts of our brain. Each section holds important information. The more information that we have about something, the more vivid and accurate that picture is.

Another benefit is that the more vivid or precise information we have, the longer we will remember it. Although we may remember something for a year, it is likely that we will retain it far more if we experience the same thing with all of our senses.

In this chapter, we will be learning a lot more about the various styles and types that are used to learn. Which learning style will work best for you and your needs? You'll have to discover for yourself. As we mentioned, everyone is different. Different people learn better using different methods.

The key isn't to find the best general method for everyone; rather, it's about finding the best individual method. What works for you is what matters most. This should not be the case for your friends and neighbors. You can listen to the opinions of others but your final decision must be based upon what is most effective for yourself.

The Principal Types of Learning

It is possible to learn about things in many different ways. You don't have to learn the exact same way every time, but there are many ways you can learn. This will help you design your learning system in a way that allows you to retain information longer and helps you learn more quickly.

Visual Learning - Reading

This is probably the most widely used way to learn. A book, article or other written matter is the best way to learn about a subject.

Written word allows us to easily explain any subject to a broad range of people. A book can be written and millions can access it.

Written word is intended to use pre-determined meanings of words in order to convey thoughts. Each word in a book is already known because we knew it before. Because we are familiar with the meaning of the word "cat", we can see a picture or image of a cat when the author uses the word. If the author does not explain what a cat is before using the term in the book, then we won't be able to comprehend.

Because it is a single-dimensional form of learning, written words are limited. We must interpret the information in our minds. In order to make it easier for people to learn, the written word is often accompanied by other learning forms.

Common forms for writing would include text books, textbooks, magazines, research papers and articles.

Visual Learning - Imitation

Sometimes we learn from others by copying their actions and learning from them. This is a common way to learn new skills and get a job. This is how children learn to play sports or do simple tasks when they're younger.

A coach will demonstrate how to hold the baseball, throw it and run correctly. The coach will then teach us how to mimic their actions until we do them right. Unfortunately, this method can cause us to pick up bad habits and not follow the correct procedures. It is always a good idea that you learn from a variety of people and combine what you are taught and learned.

Auditory Learning

Hearing can be an effective way to learn because it allows us to hear more than just the words. Although the written word might give us the meaning, the spoken words will convey the emotions.

Thus, words spoken in fear will contain not only their contents but also the emotion of fear. This makes everything look more complete and real than just the printed word.

Audio recordings, books on tape and multi-media presentations are some examples of auditory materials.

Physical Learning

Learning by doing, also known as physical learning, is a highly effective method of learning. This means that one performs or displays a specific skill or knowledge. This learning method is effective because it engages more of the senses and provides an immersive experience in learning.

It's not just a chance to learn the skill; you can also perform it, touch and experience it. You can see and feel the skill, which makes it much easier for you to remember. You must understand that not every lesson can be learned. Understanding some things requires that you experience them.

I can talk all day about how to determine if a bolt, nut, or bolt is properly tightened. But until you place a wrench on the item and actually tighten it, you'll never feel what it feels.

This is the most common type of learning. It is possible to enhance and retain the knowledge by allowing participants to practice and use the skills.

Experiencing Events

While this may seem similar to physical education, learning by experiencing is far more effective than learning from books. This is because it exposes the learner to an entire experience or situation. This allows you to comprehend a subject in far more detail and to also experience its effects as they happen.

This is important as we get feedback, which helps us to understand better and make decisions for the future. It is not possible for you to do this in a classroom. Discussion might be helpful, but it will be much more rewarding to actually experience this.

Through our daily experiences, we learn every day. This is how so many people learn, even though they don't know what they are learning. Experiments are an excellent way to teach inter-personal skills as well as how we interact with and get along.

Repetition

Sometimes you learn something by simply doing it over and over until it becomes a routine. To master a skill, you should practice it over and again until you have mastered them. This will enable you to be quick and accurate in your responses.

One example is an athlete learning how the basketball is shot from a particular position. The shot is repeated hundreds of times until the muscles in their brain know what action will result in making the shot correct. Soon, this becomes automatic and becomes a reflexive action. This allows the player speed up and is more accurate.

The benefit of repetition training is the ability to speed up the completion of tasks. For example, changing the oil in your vehicle might take you half an hour the first time around. However, after repeating the process four or five times, you can complete the task in just 20 minutes. You have done it many times and you know how to do it well.

Your life will show you many things you can do more quickly than when you attempted it. Because you are familiar with the task, repetition is key.

Trial & Error

Last but not least: We often learn from trial and error. We can see something that needs doing or make a decision. Common sense helps us to decide what the best answer is. We take action, and then we see what happens. If it works, great. We'll figure out why it doesn't and then we'll be all the wiser.

As much as inventors use the trial-and error method, so do researchers and anyone who needs to find ways to solve problems and improve on existing ones. There are always conditions or things we don't know about that must be considered. This is one way to learn.

The most common types of learning are discussed in this chapter. These will be discussed more in the future, but it's important to understand how learning works and what methods we use. Also, we should realize that all learning styles can be combined to make the most of our learning experience.

Learning by doing

I believe learning by doing. Nothing beats practicing what you're learning. It is not always easy to make mistakes and get an unacceptable result at first, but as you progress in your learning process, your results will improve.

Many times, I have sat down on my workbench with a guide on one hand and an instrument on the other. From there, I repaired or upgraded the equipment or replaced it without any special training. I have also been able to learn a lot about woodworking, home repair and other skills by doing certain things myself.

Learning by doing can be one of the most effective learning methods. While you see and hear what is happening, you also feel the emotions and sensations associated with what you're doing. Your brain processes all the information to build a vast knowledge base.

When you try something, you'll find you get better results. You will also notice a faster completion rate for projects and tasks if you try more. Because your brain and muscles form a memory about what is required to get the best results, and your skills and abilities become better over time. An hour-long project that took three hours initially with only marginal results could soon take just one hour with great results. All of this comes down to a steady improvement in your skills.

Learning by doing is a wonderful way to learn new things. You should also be aware that there are some important things to keep in mind. These are just a handful:

You must accept the risk

When you're trying something for the first-time, ensure the risk to yourself as well as others is acceptable. It is one thing to fix the bathroom faucet or your kitchen, but quite another to try to make your parachute.

You shouldn't "learn," about anything that could pose a risk to your financial, safety, or health. Because there are very few things you can do to make your car safer or improve its mechanical condition, you may want to try changing the oil. However, it is not a good idea to attempt to repair your dashboard's computer or disassemble the engine without having the necessary training and experience.

You can still practice with your toaster, but not the gas stove or furnace. Last but not least: Never put your safety at threat by performing tasks you're not capable of. That includes avoiding high-voltage electricity, as well as working at unsafe heights. News is filled with stories about people who are well intentioned but have been injured or killed because they don't know how to do it.

Make sure that you have the ability

Even simple tasks require some competency. You have the skills to be able to learn new things. While you might not know how oil is changed in your car, you are familiar with basic hand tools and can identify the correct direction to tighten or loosen bolts. It can be difficult to perform simple tasks like changing the oil in your car.

These skills are not impossible to learn. It is important to master the basics before you can complete any tasks. Start small, get started with the basics, and then work your way up to more difficult things at your own pace.

Before you make a decision, know the downside

Ok, so now that we've established that we have basic skills, or at least the rudiments of them, we need to understand what the consequences might be if we make a mistake. Although we can't guarantee success, it is important that we understand the potential consequences if our efforts don't pay off.

It might be worth investing a few thousand dollars in order to get a feel for the stock market. It wouldn't make sense to put all your retirement savings into one stock, even if you know it will be the winner.

Ask yourself, "If I completely fail, will I be able to withstand the consequences and costs of my actions?" Everyone makes mistakes as part of the learning process. It's only natural that we know what risks exist and what the possible downsides are.

Prepare a Fall Back Plan

It's helpful to know who to call for assistance if you find yourself in a bind or are unable to complete a task. You might turn to a neighbour, friend, or local person for help.

If you accidentally damage your car while you are working on it, you can take it into your local service centre and have it repaired. Hire a professional painter/finisher to repair any damage that you have done. Most things can be redone or replaced. If the item cannot be replaced or redone, you should hire a professional because the risk of injury is too high.

But, be careful. If you decide to attempt something, and need to have someone else redo or fix it, expect to pay a premium. It is much more difficult to fix something that has already been fixed than it is to fix something just broken. Other things may need to have their place, be checked out, or adjusted. That takes time.

Take Your Time

Learning by doing is an ongoing process and not a singular event. The goal is to learn and not to see how fast your can accomplish the task. This is not a race for the finish, but to understand the process and to complete it quickly. Take your time and understand why you are doing what you are. Take your time, understand what it is like to do the task at hand and pay attention to what happens along the way. The more you notice, the better your overall results.

Actually, you might find that it will take you much longer to do something new for the first attempt. You have to remember that everything you do is new and a little confusing the first time. The next time, you'll feel at ease and know what to do. You spend more time doing than reading or consulting manuals and more time actually performing the task.

It doesn't mean you are an expert at something. It is important to continue learning and improving your skills. You will see better results in less time when you do this task more often.

Learning by doing is a good way to learn. However, it must not be dangerous or put our safety at danger. Keep a realistic perspective of your skills and knowledge. Never try anything that poses a serious risk to you.

You might take longer to do something than a professional. Painting a room in your house might take you 3 days, while professional painters might finish it in just an hour. You don't have to give up on your dream, but this is something you need to keep in mind. Turning to a professional is a good option if time is a concern.

It is possible to learn new skills if there are resources available and you have the time and desire to practice them.

Learning by observation

Watching someone else do something is one of the best ways to learn. Then we can either follow their example or create our own method of doing the exact same thing.

This is very effective as it adds more dimensions to the lessons we are trying. The words you use to describe something can be all that you have. A picture or two can add a dimension to the story, but it is not enough.

We can see, hear, and experience everything in 3D when we are actually there to witness it. We not only watch, but we actually experience it. Additionally, sometimes we can get things more clearly and vividly explained if it is an actual learning experience.

When it comes to learning skills, classes and seminars are very popular. Home Centers offer demonstrations of how to plant a garden and build tables, as well as advanced projects like adding a roof over your home. Although it might seem difficult, these tasks are generally much simpler than they appear. It's important to have someone help you break down the tasks and demonstrate them for your benefit.

Sometimes the demonstrations might be broadcast on television. Even though it's not as clear and easy to follow as seeing in person, this can help make the process much easier. Although you won't get all of the sensory inputs that are available, you will get the majority. This can often give you enough information and skills to get you started.

The majority of us are visual people. We love to look at things. We are more interested in seeing something done than reading about it. We are action-oriented, and we believe in taking action. It is possible to learn more quickly if we are shown the material, not just read it.

There are entire cable networks dedicated solely to educational programming. The possibilities are endless when it comes down to what can be captured on film or digital. Video allows you to view even advanced topics such as medicine or technology.

It is a great way to learn by reading about the topic, then following up with a live demonstration or video. A video can bring the topic to life.

Just like with other forms of learning we need to make sure that the person who is doing the demonstration is properly trained. Do not allow someone to teach you something completely wrong. It is important to learn the correct way to do something if you are being taught the incorrect way.

You can learn by watching another person in live situations. This gives you the chance to ask questions. You can ask the instructor why it is done this way. Visual demonstrations can often bring up a lot of questions as we observe how it is done and think of alternative ways.

Sometimes these alternatives work better and make life easier, but sometimes they don't work due to something that we overlook. A demonstration in real time is beneficial because you are able to ask questions, gain additional insight, and share your thoughts.

Learning through observations can be done in lectures, seminars or live classroom sessions. You can learn so much from any activity or document that you are able to see it in action.

Learning by listening

Many people love to learn by listening. This can be done by listening or watching audio, instructional or educational videos, or listening to books on tape which transform printed material into audio recordings.

It is possible to learn by listening without having to read. Audio is a great way to learn, especially if you are having trouble reading or just don't want to read.

For example, think about someone who drives half an hour to work every day. They might commute on the subway or train, so reading isn't an option. One cannot read a novel and also watch the roads at the same time. There are still a few hours each day when you can listen to audio.

You can learn almost anything you want with the advent of books-on-tape and small, compact MP3 players. Listen while riding, driving, waiting in a doctor's chair, or even jogging on the track to lose weight.

Whatever the application, you can find audio resources about the topics you're interested in. The audio files can be loaded into your MP3 Player or put them in your CD player at work. To ensure that you are not disturbing others, you can use headphones.

However, listening is only half the battle. You need to pay attention to the words and imagine what they are saying. Translate the words into mental images, and you will be able to understand their message. If you have difficulty understanding the words, rewind and listen to again.

The great advantage of audio learning over a lecture is the ability to rewind or re-listen to an audio file more than once. You can learn as fast or slow as you wish and can stop to re-listen to the audio several times to get the full understanding of the content.

Repeat the process until you are comfortable with the content. Do not skip the previous lesson or chapter if it is unclear. Make sure to go back over the material once more times until you get it right. Next, you can move on to chapter or next concept when you are done.

Another great advantage of audio learning is that you can play the exact same CD or MP3 over-and-over until you're familiar with it. It is a great way to embed the material in your brain by playing a CD on the road and listening to it for several weeks. It will be easier to retain it if you listen to it over and again. This is an excellent way to review and study for a test.

What happens if the audio materials you require are not available? It doesn't necessarily mean you can't use audio to make your point. Nearly every computer can record audio. You also have many audio converters to help you convert the files to MP3 for your MP3 player.

We all know that it is beneficial to read aloud and listen as we read. So why not combine both of these tasks? As you are writing or reading, turn the microphone on and record it as an audio file. That audio file can be played on any device, so you can listen to what you have learned wherever you are.

This method is especially useful for technical content and other items that require a lot memory. However, this can also be applied to everyday content. Finding as many ways to stimulate your brain's learning centers is the key. Learning by using audio certainly is one!

Learning by trial & error

If you find anyone in this book who claims to not have made a single mistake, I will be able to show you someone who is totally out of touch. Although we all make mistakes, there are some that are more common than others. It is how we deal with these mistakes that makes all the difference.

When learning is concerned, sometimes it is just as important that you learn the things that don't work. Learning negative things is a way to gain an understanding that can be crucial for grasping the concept or skill fully.

Thomas Edison was one of the world's most prolific inventors. He claimed that invention is 99% perspiration, 1% inspiration. He tried hundreds more designs while working on the electric lightbulb. When he was asked his opinion about these failures, the man replied that they were not failures. This was because he now had 100's more designs that didn't work and could cross those off his wish list.

This means that he now knows what won't work and can focus his efforts on other things.

Learning can sometimes mean learning from both failure and success. Sometimes, we learn from our mistakes and that it's not a failure. Many things in life require us to fail to learn and improve.

The child is learning to walk. They will fall every time they attempt the first step. After taking the first step, they move on to the next. That's failure helping us turn failure to success.

The same rules apply to young baseball players trying to learn how they can hit. They miss their first few swings wildly, but they then get closer and closer. They hit the ball one out of every ten swings. Then they hit it three out of ten times. They are able swing faster, or quicker, and can also coordinate their eyes and arms. It is a learning process that uses failure to help us get better.

To master almost all of the things we learn, it will take some practice and understanding. We will make errors and misjudgments along the way, as well as experience setbacks. This should not cause alarm or concern as it is part of learning. While some of us learn faster and make fewer mistakes, others take longer and make many more mistakes. It is important that we learn and not how fast it takes.

While we don't want this book to be a repeat of ourselves, it is important that we understand that we can only learn from mistakes or trial and errors. The lower the risk, better. If we are involved with something important or of significant value, it is best to take steps that minimize losses or risks.

It is one thing for a person to change the ingredients in a recipe. However, it is quite another to attempt to improve your car's fuel economy by making adjustments to the onboard computer system. It doesn't matter how good the recipe is, it will just taste wrong.

You could be charged a couple hundred dollars for the repair of the cars onboard computer. This is why you might want to take your car to someone who has a good understanding of the on-board computer systems. They can then discuss the proposed changes. They can give you advice or complete the job for a fee. That would be the most safest.

In terms of learning, we want to stress the importance of trial and error. In many cases, there won't be any other options. If you're trying to make something or create something completely new, you must do it yourself.

Because mistakes are part and parcel of learning, you should not be afraid to fail. If you avoid making mistakes, you're not pushing yourself to the limits as much as you should. Learning from your mistakes is the key. Take them apart. To make better decisions and choices the next time, find out what went wrong.

Make mistakes to help you learn and improve your skills. It is through mistakes that we learn our weak spots. If we accept a error and do not analyze it, or if our mistakes are ignored, we will never learn and continue to make the same mistakes.

So what's a "good mistake"? Anything that helps you get closer to your goals can be considered a "good" mistake, provided that the losses are not too significant. You might try 10 different combinations to find the best, and the nine failures can help you narrow down the search to find that perfect combination. In this example, every failure was an opportunity to learn from your mistakes and move closer to success.

You can make a mistake if you try to package your parachute better and it fails to open. While you may have learned something from this experience, the cost was too high for you to continue your search for the next opportunity.

Trial and error is an excellent way to discover new areas and improve your knowledge. It is the process most of us use to learn skills and abilities the first time. We should strive to minimize our errors and learn from our mistakes.

If you learn by trial-and-error, there is no room to be egocentric. Make mistakes and learn from them.

Listening to Yourself

Have you ever seen someone talk to themselves? Or someone talking about themselves to someone else that doesn't seem real? It could be one of these. They might be using the Bluetooth headset to communicate with their phone. Or they could be learning something.

A great way to retain and learn is to read aloud what's written on the page. Reading aloud is a great way for you to retain and increase your comprehension of something.

You can do this several times. Your brain will process the information twice. It first processes it as you are reading it. It then turns what you're reading into words so you can say them aloud. After that, your brain interprets what it hears and creates a memory bank.

You can increase the chance of your brain processing the same information repeatedly by reading it aloud.

The best way to use this method is to go through a book chapter by chap and then return to the beginning to read the next chapter. This will increase your brain's exposure to the material, and will help you retain it.

This is a good way to memorize any information you need. Just keep repeating the words you want to recall. Repeating the same process over and again will help you retain more information.

This doesn't just cover printed matter, but also what you might see or hear in a video or television. It works with any thoughts you may have. These thoughts can be expressed verbally, expanded upon, and even created more detailed. You may prefer to write these things down but sometimes this is not possible. If that happens, you'll need to tap into your memory to save those ideas, thoughts, and other information.

While this might seem like a straightforward way to learn but don't underestimate the value of such a method. This may be the best way to learn.

It does not have to be simple, it just has to work.

Note it!

We've just discussed how important it is to speak what you are trying to learn so your mind can process the material in more than one way. The more information we can process, the easier it is to remember and learn. Writing is another tool you have to help make learning more efficient and quicker.

Most people believe that the main reason we keep notes or write down things is to be able to refer back later if we forget something we've just heard, thought, or seen. It is true that this is a compelling reason to make a written record. But, writing increases our ability and knowledge.

Writing down information is a way to make sense of the information or learn it. It is essential that you have a basic understanding about what you are writing. This will help you choose the words to use when you write down the summary of or high points.

Second, we must convert these words to a physical movement. This is another way in which our brains process the information we are reading.

As we write, we check that our words are correct and are correctly spelled. Third, we not only write the words but also read them back, process them in our brains, and embed them deeper into ourselves.

Many educational institutions encourage students take notes and to write summaries. Not to be a burden on their time but to increase the amount of information they have learned and to retain the material longer.

It is also possible to write down the highlights and high points of the topic that you feel are most important for you. Every person is unique, so the way we view or interpret something will differ. A written record of our opinions on the most important aspects of any subject will help us in our quest to learn more about it and improve our lives.

When you next find something you want to know, make a written summary. Write down the entire text. It is important to understand the subject before you can put it in your own words. It doesn't matter what level of understanding you have. What we really want is to be capable of understanding the content, putting it in your own words and being able then to record it for future reference.

You can also refer to your notes at a later time to help you remember details or to clarify a sequence that has become confusing over the years. It is much easier to refer back to the notes you have made on a particular subject than to go through the entire subject over again. You will be able to recall more quickly and learn more easily.

Repetition

We've covered some of the most efficient and popular methods of learning and how to combine them for even greater effectiveness. The best way to increase brain learning is by stimulating the most learning centres. Learning is best when you are able to repeat the material repeatedly.

You might do this by reading the same text several times, and then processing it in a variety of ways. Repetition can be the best way for us to absorb what we have learned and make it a part of our brains.

It is easier to remember something if we do it repeatedly. The ultimate result is the ability to perform tasks faster, better, and more quickly than others.

You have a few options to help you remember and retain information. You can improve your recall by using a different format. This could be reading first, then alouding the second time and then writing a summary. You can increase your recall and comprehension by using a new format.

Repetition can be a huge help with physical skills. While it may take you an hour for a task to be completed the first time, you will soon find yourself completing the task in half the time if you keep going back over the process multiple times. It is because of confidence and ability that has replaced hesitation and needing to consult notes.

You must be aware of one important fact about repetition. Effective repetition is key to success. If you are trying to cut corners or do things the wrong way to save some time, it will just make your skills more skilled at doing things wrong. It will take more effort to train your brain so it forgets what you were doing, and does things the right-way.

Although you may think you know everything, it doesn't mean that you shouldn't try the process again to become more comfortable. It is important to remember that tasks can be both simple or complex and that advanced skills are more valuable than our basic skills. Don't rush, take your time and make sure you don't forget what you learned. Only then should it be time to move on.

Break it Down

Perhaps you have ever attempted to tackle a difficult project or to learn something complex. We can sometimes feel overwhelmed by the scope of the task that we give up and quit before we even get started. This means that we don't get the information we need. This is a common problem but there are effective and easy ways to deal with it.

Each task or challenge is complex and requires many steps. The act of getting water and drinking it is one example. To begin, reach for the glass. Then, hold the glass in your hand, lift it, and then open your mouth. This is a very simple task and takes only 7 steps. If you fail to follow the seven steps, you will most likely have to clean up water spilled.

Consider if drinking is a simple task and requires seven steps. Then think about how many steps it might take for you to become a doctor, master a new skill or repair your car engine. It might take 700, 7000 or more steps to reach your goal. Sometimes, the greatest and most dedicated people can give up when they realize the enormity of what lies ahead.

What would happen if you broke the whole thing down into smaller manageable pieces. What might be our attitude if each one of these pieces was simpler and more manageable? Would it make us more likely to stay focused on the task and be motivated?

Consider the following example:

Let's say that you wanted to be a physician or lawyer. You might be skeptical about the process. There would be 8 years of schooling and 4 years of residency. You might feel motivated to start, but the enormity and complexity of the task ahead could crush your spirit.

You might find it easier to keep motivated and apply yourself if you break it into 12 steps. This year could be treated as a project or task. If you can identify the objectives, rewards and responsibilities associated with each year, things will be much easier to manage.

You will also be able to easily see the real progress. Looking at all the details, you'd see that your first year was a success. One year down, 7 more to go. The overall task is just too overwhelming to manage early on.

If you could just say "OK!" at the end, it would be a great thing. That's it. One year is done. I'm done with step one. It was completed on time. I'm able to now use my skills to volunteer on the ambulance. It will give me some valuable experience which will come in handy later. I am making great progress!"

It is enough to be able to see real progress and to feel motivated. The work involved and the time it takes will remain the same. But how we look at it is different. We don't see a single daunting and intimidating task ahead. Instead, we see a series small and manageable issues that we are better equipped for.

These two examples are at opposite ends of the spectrum. Any task we want to complete, or any subject we want to master, can be broken down into manageable steps. Chapters can be used to break down books. Instead of looking at

600 pages as too long, try to think of it as 18 chapters. You will need to dedicate a week each chapter. The goal of reading 50 pages is easier than 800.

It is important to keep your goal in sight and make it as easy as possible. It doesn't mean you should do everything in record time. Faster isn't always better when it comes to learning. It is possible to learn things quickly in order to meet a deadline, or to complete a task on schedule. However, the best learning happens when you are organized and take the time to absorb and process the information.

When you're faced with a daunting task and need to learn something new, you can use a pen and paper to break it down into smaller steps. It is important to establish a time frame for each step and give yourself goals.

It will result in a less stressful and manageable process that will lead to you reaching your goal, learning new skills or learning something valuable in your life. Concentrate on the steps you need to take to achieve your goal. This should be the main motivator. If this helps, then you should do it. It doesn't signify that you lack intelligence or are not interested in maximizing your chances of success.

It is up to you to decide how long it should take.

Making it Relevant

Sometimes the human brain is funny. It likes to do things that provide a benefit and avoids tasks that feel inefficient or not worth its time. We are wired to believe our efforts will be worthwhile to achieve the best results.

Sometimes, even though all that is well and good, we may have to learn something that doesn't make sense or give us the benefit. It may be that the material is tedious or boring, which makes it even more difficult to comprehend. Last but not the least, we try not to learn or understand something that is not relevant for us or our situation.

These are all common situations in life. This is why we need to find effective ways to deal with them. There is an easy, effective way anyone can increase their ability learn and retain material.

This involves making the materials that we are trying learn directly applicable to our lives. When we take an abstract concept and turn it into something that can be used in our lives, it makes us more determined and motivated to learn it.

Let's suppose, for example that we need knowledge about customer service. We must learn this to get a better job or to improve our performance at work. Customer service training can include many different concepts and components. These concepts may not be the most fascinating, but we can benefit from learning these skills by applying them to real-world examples.

Let's say that we need to learn how conflict can be resolved. In order to resolve conflict, we need to calm the customer down. We call this a neutral position. Customers are no longer angry, upset or happy. This is the goal: to calm down customers and get them to listen and think with you, and not be affected by their emotions.

If we think about the skill or concept we are learning, and how it could be applied to difficult customer situations, or how it would have helped us with customers in our past, then we will see the value of practicing and learning that skill.

Our brains become more engaged when we make something meaningful or more personal. It's like a lightbulb going off in our brains. We realize this is going to be a big help in our daily lives. It is going make something more useful, easier, or more valuable." The brain then focuses its attention on the learning process.

This allows us to concentrate for longer periods of times and is more effective. It allows us learn more and faster. Because the materials that we are learning attach to previous memories, we are able to retain the information for longer times and often in greater detail.

Making things relevant is another way to make them more useful and clearer. While we might be able to comprehend a text when we read it, when we stop to think about how this knowledge can be applied in our lives and give examples to illustrate the point, things start to make sense and become more comprehensible.

So, now that everyone agrees that making things relevant will help you learn faster and more effectively, the big question is: How do we do it in an easy way?

You can start by thinking about the topics at the beginning. Once you have done this, you can then brainstorm examples and reasons why it will be beneficial for you. List all the reasons. Do you think it will make your life easier? It can save you money. Will it make life more fulfilling? Will it allow you to earn more? Will it make you happier? The answers to these questions can be powerful motivators.

Next, stop learning after each chapter and start thinking about how this new information can be applied in your everyday life. You can think about when and how this information might be of benefit to you. You can see how this information could make your life easier and more pleasant. You can think of instances in your life where this could have been useful.

You can imagine how you would have done things differently and what the outcome might be. Learning will improve your comprehension and retention if you discover more positive benefits.

This isn't magic. Instead, it uses one of the strengths of the human brain. It is not meant to manipulate us into doing things we don't like, but rather to make it appreciate the value of what you ask it to do. We are simply trying to get your brain on our side, and to get it learning faster and better.

Visualization

Learners take in some information. How well we process it will determine how accurate and how long it remains in our memory.

Some courses in speed reading allow people to read huge books within a matter of hours. Although speed reading may be appropriate for books that are enjoyable, it does not make sense when it comes to learning. Speed reading may be okay for some people but for most of us, speed is better than comprehension.

You should not just read a book, article, manual or other material. It should be experienced. You should listen carefully to what you are reading and make a mental picture or an image to help you understand the meaning.

Be aware that words only work as well as the meaning we assign them in our brains. When we hear the word green, we picture a green image in mind. It is because we have equated the word green to the color green. It is the same for other words like big, small, smooth, rough, and others.

We might lose the details and nuances of the information we are trying to grasp if we only read at a high-level level. While we can reduce time, meanings could also be lost.

Now, think about the sentence "The big raw red ball rolled along the hill." When you read it and absorb all the words, you will get an image of the large red and rough object rolling along the hill. It is going faster and more quickly as it goes downhill. Based on the words that you have read, this is the correct image.

However, if you read too fast or skip some words and imagine "the ball rolled up the hill", you may see a tiny ball that is slowly rolling down a hill. This image might not be accurate. It is a large ball, and could cause damage to anything it passes. It all comes down the interpretation and how you read it.

If we want to learn something we must take the time not only to read the words but also to process the meanings. It's not possible to simply read and forget the words. Instead, it is important to read and understand the words as well as the images.

Even though this sounds like a lot to do, our brains are able to handle most of this work automatically, even if we don't think about it. It's only when we try and learn too fast or fail to concentrate that we find difficulty. You may have heard the expression "went into one ear and out of the other", which refers to people who can hear and pay no attention. They see or hear, but don't process. Therefore, they don't know.

You should make sure that the image is as precise and descriptive as you can when trying to learn. You can imagine what the image will look and feel like. See it in fine detail. Is the surface smooth or rough? Is the size of the object large or small. Are they shiny or matte? Loud, soft or loud? What is the difference between light and dark? Hot or cold Easier or more difficult?

The more detail that you can associate with an item, the more vivid it is in your mind. You'll also be able to pull up this information more accurately in the future. Words are two-dimensional tools used to describe three-dimensional objects. When we read these words, our brains will convert them into the right images.

Make accurate images of what you have learned. Make sure to look at the details as well as the most crucial characteristics of each item or concept. The more details you understand, the better your education. This is often what makes the difference between knowing something well and just "kinda" knowing it.

You can think of the things you are most proud to have in your past. Those are the things that stick in your head after you've forgotten many other things. Chances you have those as your most vivid memories. You will remember the little things. You can remember how the memory made you feel and what you were doing at the time. Those are the thoughts you want to cultivate in your mind while you learn new things. To ensure that you don't forget what you have learned today but can retain it for future years.

Next time you read something, do more than just read it. Experience it. Giving words life and meaning. The perfect image should include all your senses. The more details you can give, the better you will be at it and the more you will remember what you learned.

Visualization

Learners take in some information. How accurate we are with our knowledge and how long we retain it can be directly affected by how we process it.

Some courses in speed reading allow people to read huge books within a matter of hours. Although speed reading may be appropriate for books that are enjoyable, it does not make sense when it comes to learning. Speed reading may be okay for some, but for most people it is better to sacrifice comprehension for speed.

You should experience what you are reading when you read a book, article, manual or other type of material. You should listen carefully to what you are reading and make a mental picture or an image to help you understand the meaning.

Be aware that words are only as powerful as the meanings we assign to them in our brains. We have a mental image of green when we read the word Green. It is because we have equated the word green to the color green. It is the same for other words, like big and tiny, smooth or rough, and many others.

We might lose the details and nuances of what is being learned if we only read at a high-level level. While we can reduce time, meanings could also be lost.

Now, think about the sentence "The big raw red ball rolled along the hill." When you read it and absorb all the words, you will get an image of the large red object rolling downhill at speed. It is going faster as it goes downhill. Based on the words you've read, this is the correct image.

However, if you read too fast or skip some words and imagine "the ball rolled up the hill", you may see a small, delicate ball that is simply rolling down a hill and doing its own thing. It is actually a large ball, and could cause damage to anything it passes. It all depends on how you interpret and read.

If we want to learn something we must take the time not only to read the words but also to process the meanings and create images that correspond with what we have just read. We cannot just read and forget the information. Instead, it is important to read and understand the words as well as the images.

Even though this may sound like a lot of work it's actually not. When given the chance our brains will perform most of these tasks automatically, without us even realizing. It's only when we try and learn too fast or fail to concentrate that we find difficulty. You may have heard the expression "went into one ear and out of the other", which refers to people who can hear and pay no attention. They see or hear but don't process. They don't learn.

You should make sure that the image is as precise and descriptive as you can when trying to learn. You can imagine what it looks like, feels like, how it smells, and what size it is. See it in fine detail. Is the surface smooth or rough? Is the size of the object large or small. Are they shiny or matte? Loud, soft or loud? What is the difference between light and dark? Hot or cold Easier or more difficult?

The more detail that you associate with an item, the more vivid it is in your mind. You'll also be able to pull that information up in the future more accurately. Words are two-dimensional tools used to describe three-dimensional objects. It is up our brains to transform those words into the right images when we read them.

Make accurate images of what you have learned. Make sure to look at the details as well as the most crucial characteristics of each item or concept. The more information you have, the more complete your education. This is often what makes the difference between knowing something well and just "kinda" knowing it.

You can think of the things from your past. Those are the things that stick in your head after you've forgotten many other things. These may be your most vivid memories. You will remember the little things. You can remember how the memory made you feel and what you were doing at the time. Those are what you want to hold onto as you learn more. This will allow you to learn more today and keep it in your mind for future months and years.

Next time you read something, do more than just read it. Experience it. Giving words meaning and life. The perfect image should include all your senses. The more details you can give, the better you will be at it and the longer your memory will hold what you have learned.

The Building Block Approach for Learning

Different types of skills are necessary to learn something. It is important that the learning process be structured to teach us these skills in the order that we need. If you try to learn skills without order, it's like trying to learn to run before learning to walk. You are likely to experience disappointment and frustration.

The majority of textbooks will provide the background or foundation to what you desire to learn. You want to establish a foundation of basic skills that can be used to build advanced skills. If you want to learn to build a backyard deck, then you must first learn to use a drill and a power saw. If you lack these skills, it will be difficult to build a nice deck.

First, use scrap wood to build a few smaller projects. Then you can start to master the saw/screw gun. You can then move onto more advanced skills after you have learned the basics. Mastering the basics is key to gaining a solid foundation that will allow you to move on to more difficult concepts.

People make the common mistake of looking at the basics and thinking that they already know it all. Or that these skills don't matter. Then they skip those chapters and jump to the "good stuff". Many people find themselves unable to grasp complex topics due to a lack of knowledge of the basics. You must therefore take the time to master your fundamental skills in order to be able to build upon them.

This is especially important if you're trying to learn a manual or physical skill. Sometimes you don't know enough about the basics and this can hinder your ability to complete the task efficiently. The deck example above shows that you could have the most amazing deck ever, but no one will love it if everything is wrong or the screws aren't inserted correctly.

It is best to be honest with oneself when learning the basics. Be honest with yourself if you don't understand something or "kinda" know it. Always read each chapter and segment of a book, or view the entire video, even if it seems like you have mastered something. There are many different ways to accomplish the same task. You may discover a tip that works for you or another way. Don't forget the basics!

Sometimes a book, video, seminar, or class won't cover everything. Video tutorials on how to rebuild an engine will not cover the basics of using power tools and hand tools. There is a good chance that you will struggle to use hand and power tools for the first time.

You must be open with yourself before you can learn anything. Get the skills you need to tackle advanced subjects. It is well-worth the effort and will make it easier to move on.

You have the basics covered. Now it's time learn more and add some knowledge or skills to them. Advanced skills will make it easier as they are generally just slightly more complex and well-defined skills that require you to use material you already know. These advanced skills are added on to the basics and suddenly you're more proficient.

Be sure to feel confident with the material you've just learned before moving onto the next chapter. It will be less effective to try and learn new skills on top or develop skills you already have. While some may think that this is a waste, in reality it saves you time and is much more beneficial in the long-term.

Be sure to use your new knowledge in the right manner. Avoid taking shortcuts or trying to cut corners. This is especially true when you're performing any type of physical task. Building blocks learning is great because you'll be practicing your skills and also improving on old ones. As you build your second deck, you will improve your accuracy with the saw and speed up with the screw gun.

However, if you do not follow the correct procedure or use shortcuts because it is easier or you don't know the details well enough to fully grasp it at the time you learn it, this will result in inaccurate knowledge that you can repeat as you progress and may cause other skills to suffer. You should take your time, be thorough and carefully monitor your learning progress.

One of the best methods for learning is building block learning. Even though it might be something you haven't noticed or thought of, it is all around. Building block learning will help you achieve great heights in the learning process if you take your own time and progress only when you are ready.

It's a learning process that requires focus, discipline and honesty. Do not proceed until you are confident that you have the basics mastered. Learn each skill one at a time before moving onto the next.

Being honest in your evaluations and remaining committed to the process will ensure that you are successful and have knowledge that is accurate, complete and ready for you to use throughout your lifetime.

Video Learning

Today almost every skill can be taught by video. Videos can be searched on any topic. There are many ways to quickly access videos. You have your computer that gives you the internet and sites like YouTube. And you have your home DVD player, or portable video device that brings your videos to wherever you may need them.

Videos are great for learning. It is much easier to learn a musical instrument if you can watch it being played. This doesn't translate well to book format at times. It is important to be able see how to hold an instrument and what a decent sounding note looks like so you can determine what your final result should sound.

This is similar to what you would get in a music lesson. It's easy to see how it works and hear the final result. If your final result sounds exactly the same as the ones shown, it means that you are capable to complete the task.

Any task that requires action, such repairing or building something, or using a tool or instrument, can be taught via video. Even printed materials can be transposed into video, and people can speak or act out the information in a visual format.

You must take reasonable steps, just like with any other type of learning. The fact that someone has made a video does NOT mean they are proficient in doing the task. Note that the same applies to writing a novel.

Video learning is an effective method of learning because it involves multiple brain regions. To really get the feeling of the content and the procedure, we can both see it and hear it.

Video can be effective because not all things are easily translated into words. For example, a picture of someone playing a guitar chord can be more helpful than 3 paragraphs explaining which finger is where on the neck.

It is said that a picture speaks louder than a thousand words. That is because we can get so much information from one photo. We can see things in context and how they compare to other things. It is possible to see how something should look and how to adjust it or hold it.

Visual aids such video and pictures are not only a powerful way to communicate, but they can also make learning much easier, quicker, and more effective. Give a video a shot if you've never tried learning something through video. Sometimes, you can learn a lot more in five minutes than you can in three hours of reading a text book.

Distractions

People fail to learn when they do not have the right environment. It's not because people are not smart enough or dedicated enough. People set themselves up for failure when they try to learn in an environment which doesn't allow them to concentrate on the learning process.

Distractions distract us from the task of orderingly transferring materials from videos and books into our brain. The brain needs to be able to work efficiently and effectively so that it is at its best. It should operate like a well-oiled machine. Interruptions cause the machine to stop and then it must wait until it regains its speed.

Some people are able learn with external distractions. But even those people, it will take them longer to learn. The simple truth of the matter is that quality results are more likely to be produced if we can focus on the task at hand.

With this in mind, here are some tips on how to create the best learning environment possible:

Dedicate Time

By putting aside time for learning, you'll get better results. It means you should set aside specific time each day for learning. Do not schedule appointments. Don't allow phone calls. Let everyone know that this is your learning or training time.

Now, I know that exceptions in real life will need to be made. Emergencies happen, situations require attention, and people are sick or in need of special treatment. These things happen and they shouldn't be avoided. It is important to communicate to those around us that we have spoken and that they should respect our wishes.

Studies show that people who devote time and allow for flexibility in their lives get better results. People who try and fit everything in at the last moment often put things off until next week, next month or next year. Don't let yourself fall for this trap.

It is important to set aside time for learning. While there is no limit to how long you can spend learning, I recommend no less than 30 mins and no more than three hours. You won't be able to learn in the learning mode for less than 30 mins.

While it's better that nothing, it is not significantly better.

Marathon sessions don't often work. We get tired and our brains stop taking in information for too long. You will be more productive scheduling several shorter sessions than one longer session. You'll be more alert, more open and more willing to learn.

Also, this should be the most time you can spend learning every week or month. Do you ever feel the need for reading or to watch a movie at other times? This is the minimum amount of time you need to devote each week in order to stay on track and reach your goals.

Establish a Reasonable Pace

A common mistake that people make is to push too hard. We must take our time and learn at a pace that suits us. This is not the way to go for your friend, colleague or brother. Each learns at their own pace. It might take some of us two days to finish a novel, while others could take months. You can't be right or wrong.

It is important to choose a pace which allows you to complete the material in a reasonable time frame, yet still leaves you with enough time to fully understand and process it. Comprehensiveness is more important that speed. It is not a race for the finish. It's not the person who finishes first that is important, but rather the person who has the greatest understanding and highest level skills.

Eliminate Interruptions

Uninterrupted time is crucial for learning. We want our minds to focus on what is happening and the information coming in. If we are continually interrupted by phone calls and messages, e mails, or other communications, it will slow down our ability to learn.

We need to communicate with those around that we expect to not be interrupted during sessions, unless there is an actual emergency. We need to close our e mail screens, turn off our phones and get rid any other distracting information that might be in our way.

We must remain firm and refuse to make exceptions unless absolutely necessary. Most emergencies can wait until you're done with your session. This should be understood by everyone. They need to know that you are serious and dedicated to your learning.

Be Quiet

It is easier to learn and retain information in a quiet, relaxed environment. It is easier to learn in 20 minutes at home than in 20 minutes in a busy subway car.

Turn off the TV, and listen to MP3

Studying while listening to music or watching TV is a common habit. Both of these are bad habits. Even though we may not realize it, our brains process the sounds we hear. This can distract us from the content we are reading and watching.

You will get the best results and the fastest possible time if you are fully focused on what you are learning. You must cut out everything that distracts from what you are doing.

TV can be dangerous as we can become distracted by what's on the screen. It might be something that catches our attention first, then we start to look at the screen and before you know it, you're watching the program while reading for the next 30 minute!

Some music is relaxing, but can also be dangerous. To see if this is possible, you might be able to learn with out the use of music. Be careful to not let music dominate your learning sessions if you do need it.

Get Organized

You will avoid being interrupted and losing your time. Make sure that you have all the necessary items at hand. It is important to have all the necessary tools at your disposal, including pencils and notebooks, software, videos, pennies, pencils, and even video. Interruptions lead to lost time.

Set aside time for learning, and make sure others are aware. This time period is yours to control, so make the most of them.

The Learning Environment

It is important to make learning enjoyable and successful. The goal is to have everything you need at your fingertips and to create learning environments that are easy.

Nothing beats silence when it comes concentration. If your children are shouting at each other and your spouse is talking on the telephone or watching TV, you won't be able focus well. Your train of thinking will be disrupted, and it will take some time to get your thoughts back on track.

Do your best for a peaceful place far from the daily hustle and bustle. It accomplishes two things. It allows you to concentrate and makes it difficult for others to reach out to you.

This might be done at home in the office, basement, or both. You might use a conference space or an empty office for this purpose at work. Do not attempt to learn while sitting at your desk. People will assume you're working when you're not there. They may ask you questions, give other work, or otherwise distract from your learning. Your phone rings constantly at the worst times, which can lead to a serious problem.

Your work area should be suitable in size and layout for what you're doing. It should be large enough for you to read the book, and enough space to keep your notepaper. If you are trying to learn a new skill or process, your work area should be large enough that you can also store the tools and other materials you will need.

Lighting is crucial because it can make your eyes strain and cause you to lose your ability to focus or read. This will result in you not being able to work as hard and eventually, it will lead to headaches that will make it nearly impossible to concentrate.

Lighting is essential when you perform tasks. It will be necessary to be able look at what you are doing as well as the results. Lighting can be dimmed or blocked, making it difficult or impossible for you to see everything. Sometimes it can be difficult to see all areas so make sure that you have a flashlight or a light source nearby.

Sometimes, we may need additional resources to help us learn new things. These may include text books and reference texts such as service manuals, videos, or other resources. You will save a lot time if these resources are available at all times. Every time you have to get up to look for something, it is time lost.

Your learning area will largely be based on common sense. But what happens if you are forced to learn by circumstances? Maybe your boss insists you stay at work. Maybe your home is small and you don't have a dedicated space for learning. You might also find it difficult to learn while on your commute to work.

These are just a few examples of a poor training area. You can make the best of a difficult situation by learning how to adapt.

You should first get noise cancelling headphones. These headphones filter out all noises around us, making the environment quieter. These filters work well on airplanes as they remove the engine hum. You can still use them on the bus or at work to aid in learning.

You can read your material on a small device such as a Nook or Kindle if you're in a tight spot like on a train, bus, or train. This will make it much easier to read, and also save you from having to carry around heavy books all the time. One reader can store hundreds, so resources and manuals may be able to be kept there.

To help you organize your materials and keep them organized, whether you're learning in multiple places or on the go, consider buying a tote or bag. This will allow you to easily grab everything and take it with you wherever you go. It will be easy to forget something, or worry about missing something.

If you're like me and are learning or training while on the move, be sure to keep your reading glasses handy in your learning bag. Your reading glasses on the train or bus will not be of any use, so don't leave them on your desk at work and on your end table at home.

What Works For You?

In learning, we all have our own unique strengths and weaknesses. We all have our strengths and weaknesses, and we are better at certain things than others. It only makes sense that some learning methods might prove more beneficial for us than others, such as our neighbors, co-workers, and friends.

A common mistake that many people make, as well as educational institutions, is believing that if something works for one person it will work equally for all. It might be true that it may partially be true. However, some people will benefit more if they learn the best and most efficient methods.

I've always been a visual person. For example I like to watch and learn by seeing and doing. I love to read, and I read several books each week. But visual is my best method of learning a skill, or improving a talent.

Friends of mine love to read books. They have a natural talent for learning from books and are able to absorb a lot of information that is not easily found in other people. They are able to read and digest 600 pages, but they don't care about what you or I do. However, this works best for them.

These examples may not be right or wrong, but neither is the other. These examples are just observations about what works best for the people who use them. It is important that we understand what works best so we can focus on learning and learn faster. It is not about being right, but about getting the best results.

Sometimes people are just not able to understand what you're going through and think that if they learned one way, it would work for them. This is not uncommon among relatives and parents. They don't intend to cause harm or discourage you. They simply want to be there to offer guidance. They should encourage you to use your strengths in the way that works best for you.

That doesn't mean you have to say, "Reading isn't for me, so it's not for me anymore." It's a foolish attitude and a false statement. It is impossible to see all the information on an audio or video file. There is a lot of information that can only be read or in writing. You are simply foolish to say you will ignore all that information and the potential benefits it could bring you is absurd.

Instead, try every type of learning you can to find what works well for you and what does not. When you do this, you will be able choose the most appropriate learning method for you.

If you want to learn the basics of guitar playing and are visual learners, then you might rent or buy a DVD. You can also watch videos on YouTube. If this was not available, then you might consider purchasing a book that teaches how to play the guitar. First, choose the one that works for you. If it's not, go to number 2 or 3.

Sometimes, we may just want to take the fastest route to success and then add another level of learning to expand our knowledge. You don't have any excuse not to combine methods to get better results.

I don't like shortcuts and trying to find the fastest way out. But I don't mind working harder than I need to. I'd be foolish to waste twice as much time on the same task if it can be done in half the time. With this in mind, wouldn't it make more sense to discover what works for yourself and not try to copy what worked for someone else.

Try out each popular form of learning. Discover what you are most drawn to.

Take a rental video, borrow a tape or read a book to find out what you liked the most. Enjoyment is more important than being unable to stand things. It's not necessary to use learning as an excuse.

Take Notes

When it comes to learning, we've already mentioned how important it is to use more of our senses. It is vital to not only learn, but also to be able to visualize and experience the information in our minds. We also talked about how decompressing things can improve our memory and retention.

There is another reason that taking notes and writing summaries may be beneficial.

Sometimes, when we learn something new, we are expected to process many different pieces and often in a particular order. Even after we've learned all we can, there are still things that might seem a bit unclear or fuzzy.

Not only are they great for improving your memory, but also give you a way to keep track of all the information so that you can go back whenever you need. You can then refer back to the notes if you have any questions or confusions.

This works well when learning complex technical material, such as formulas or equations, and procedures that need to be performed in a specific order. Because we forget things we don't use frequently, keeping notes and records can help us re-learn them.

One professor said at the beginning of each lecture that we would rarely require formulas and equations. He would also talk about them that day. He did warn us, however, that they could be hard to locate so we should make sure to note them down. I wasn't in need of them for many years. Then one day, I needed them again and I knew where to find them. Make sure you take notes and keep a record of what you have learned.

When you are preparing for an interview or a test, it is a good idea to have notes and summaries. Instead of reading through entire books and then wasting time, review your notes to refresh you memory and prepare for the test.

If you take notes, it is important to keep them all together and to date them. You will know where the parts you need when you go back to them. It's not good to lose important information or have no idea where it is located among 47 notebooks. Not all items need to be labeled daily. However, a weekly or monthly label will greatly assist in finding the right notebook. At the very least, limit it to a handful of items.

Multi-Format Learning

This topic has been covered before, but we wanted to expand on multi-format education. Multi-format Learning is the merging of two or more learning forms to increase understanding and comprehension of what we are learning.

Looking back at your "younger years", you will see that you learned about something from a text book, and then watched a video or movie about the same or related content. This was not done to waste your time or give a break to the teacher (OK. Some teachers did use videos to break ...)), but rather to provide the student with another way to process what they had just learned.

Combining written materials and audio and/or video is one of many ways to gain new insight, increase knowledge, and use that knowledge.

Multi-format learning enables us to learn multiple things. Some of those things include:

Learning has an additional dimension

As we already mentioned, multi-modal learning increases comprehension and retention. Combining reading and listening can help you understand what you're trying to learn.

Additional Viewpoints/Interpretation

Every time you view something in a different format, you get a different perspective. It could be something you learn from a picture or video, or something you hear in an audio file. Video and audio allow you to see and hear the emotions and inflections of voices. This is something that you cannot convey as effectively in an article or a book.

It is less likely for you to misplace something

Sometimes we forget to notice what is happening. It is why it is important to read and watch more than one video or book. Every time we watch something, we discover little things that we hadn't seen before. Maybe we were too busy focusing on other things, or perhaps we didn't pay enough attention. However, if we watch the video, read the book and practice, we will soon be more proficient and knowledgeable.

Additional Details

It's wonderful to read books, but sometimes you can gain more information by looking at a photo or hearing an explanation rather than just reading the words. Video and photos can help people see the details of what is happening. One picture or one video can show you what it looks like. But this doesn't mean there aren't places for written word and textbook learning. We are merely saying that video and photos can increase your knowledge.

Practice, Practice, and Practice

All the knowledge we acquire is useless if we do not use it. While knowledge makes us smarter, smarter, better at communicating with others, its main purpose is to be used. It's simple: if you don't use it you will lose it.

The top of our brains is where new knowledge lies. This knowledge is readily accessible and easy to recall. It stays at the topmost of our brains the longer we use it. It's easy to forget about it and make new knowledge. The "old wisdom" gets lost and is eventually covered up to the point that it's no longer possible to remember.

Two major situations are where knowledge is most useful. The first time you use knowledge is after the learning experience. These times, the knowledge is fresher and easier to access. This knowledge may have been just recently acquired or even last week. It is still fresh on our minds.

Now is the time when we can use this knowledge to expand or deepen it. This may include reading different perspectives or showing a new skill, and then practicing it to make it better. This activity is called "practice makes perfect". You'll remember it more if you practice it more.

After you have learned the skill and developed it, the second time will be after it has been used. We run the risk of forgetting or losing that knowledge if it is never used. It doesn't matter if we use the same skills every day or every month. But skills that aren't used often or at all risk can be put at risk.

You might think of riding a bicycle. When you were little, your bicycle was a joy to ride. It could be ridden up hillsides, over curbs and do tricks. You may be able remember how to ride, but twenty years later your skills have become less effective and more uncertain.

The ability to execute tasks or skills that are related to the body must be practiced. Also, practice should be done until the tasks become second nature. True craftsmen are often distinguished from laymen by their ability to execute tasks by habit.

This means that we can claim that practice and embedding the knowledge we have gained not only improves our skills but also keeps it fresh and updated. It helps us improve our learning and keeps the knowledge up-to-date for longer time periods. Even though we might not remember everything, we can forget the details and nuances that were taught in the beginning.

When you learn something new, it is a good idea that you think about how you want to use your knowledge in your daily lives. For those who are just curious about the subject, it is a good idea to revisit your materials periodically to keep your knowledge up-to-date.

Mentoring Someone

We now need to think about how to increase our knowledge and how to retain it for a longer time. We've already talked about how using something is the best way of learning and improving on it. Do you know a better way than teaching someone else how to use your new knowledge?

Transferring your knowledge to others is a great method of increasing your knowledge and retention. Take a moment to think about this. A thorough knowledge of a subject is essential in order to impart it to others. As you answer questions, your knowledge of the subject will improve. Each time you contact someone to tech them about something, the repetition of the information will help you retain it.

In order to teach something to someone else, you must present it in a way the person can understand and learn. These alternative presentations require you to put in a lot of effort. You'll find it easier to explain things and your comprehension will increase.

Teaching other people does not have to be done in a classroom. You could share the knowledge you have learned with someone else at work, family or friends. You can also work with this person to practice or apply the materials, which will help you both become better over time. You don't need to do anything difficult or complex. You can share your knowledge with others to benefit both yourself and the other person.

Mentoring or teaching others can be a great way to help others and your own self-esteem. Mentoring and teaching another human being would easily be a win/win situation.

Viewpoints, Interpretations

When it comes down to the truth, the main reason why we learn anything at all is that we want to. We are either trying to make things more efficient, better, or more valuable. We also need to learn in order to fulfill an obligation. No matter how we decide to learn something, we must ensure we know it well.

A book that covers all aspects of any subject would make learning easier. It would be awesome to have one source that taught everything in one place. The problem is that often this one magical resource doesn't exist.

A problem that we all face is the constant change in everything around us, even if we are studying or learning history. Things change faster than others but very few things we have today is the same as it was 50 years ago. Even worse, many of the things today are significantly different than 20 years ago.

It means that knowledge can change just as quickly as the things around it. In order to stay current on some subjects, it is necessary to constantly update and add to our knowledge. You will need to read more books and watch more videos. While a book 10 years old is still useful, it's bound to contain outdated information.

You should also consider the company or person who wrote the book. This person or company may see things in one way. But that is not the only view. It is important to read and view several videos about the subject in order to have a holistic education. This will expose you to different viewpoints and observations, as well different content in certain cases.

It is also helpful to read information differently. The information will also be more interesting and richer if you learn about other perspectives and things. When we see something from multiple perspectives, we gain more understanding and increase our depth of knowledge.

Rarely is there a time in our lives when everyone agrees on everything. It is rare that people will agree on the same topic or event. They may look at it differently. Who is to decide who is right and who wrong? It is possible for both to be right. But, it is impossible to know until you understand and compare both approaches.

Last, but not least: When we view a movie, read a book or learn in any format, it is assumed that the material is truthful and accurate. Sometimes this isn't the case. Sometimes the author is wrong, or they may not be able to show you how to complete a task. The information they provide may be out of date or unclear. They are just passing it on to you.

This is yet more reason why you shouldn't limit your sources of information to one book, video or other. Read more on the subject. Confirm what you just learned or were taught is accurate. Learn if there is another way or a different perspective to complete a task.

Each of us learns in our own unique way. Information comes from many sources. When we take it in, we blend it together to form our view and our approach. We combine information from different sources and create our own views and feelings on the subject. This doesn't mean that we are right or wrong. It simply means that after learning the material, we have a different view.

You shouldn't cut corners and you shouldn't stop learning once you've read a book or taken a class. Continue to learn about the subject, and from various sources. You'll find your knowledge grows deeper and more accurate with each passing day.

Isn't this the primary purpose of trying to learn more about something else?

Pro-Active Learning

Learning is something that most people do on an as-needed basis. In other words, once we understand the need for learning more about something, then we can start to plan how we will do it. It is just human nature. Sometimes there are things we know in advance but need to be taught.

When this happens, it's best to be proactive about learning.

A pro-active approach involves taking steps to learn something before it is really necessary. If you know that you'll need a skill in the next 12 months, you can either wait and see how it develops or take action now and learn.

The pro-active approach offers many benefits. These are some of the key benefits. Others may also apply.

Less Stress

There is more stress when you leave something up to the last minute. We don't have as much flexibility in scheduling and the fear of not being able to complete the task or another task on the schedule is a constant. It is distracting to have a deadline fixed over our heads all through the process.

You are free to create your own schedule

It is far better to be able work when you want. To be able fit everything into your life in the most efficient and relaxing manner possible. Unexpected time is an opportunity to lower the load and obtain better results.

A longer time frame allows us to make adjustments to our learning as necessary. With the additional time, we can fit more things into our schedule.

You can learn at your own pace

We have discussed the importance learning at the pace and speed that works for you. If you go too fast, things can get lost and materials are not learned.

Allowing ourselves more time allows us to control the speed at which we learn material.

This allows us to stop and review the material we don't quite understand and not have to move too quickly because we have to complete the task within two days. This facilitates better understanding and learning throughout the task.

Short deadlines and stressful paces can increase the chances of cutting corners and getting the job done faster, which can result in lower comprehension and poor quality learning. Sometimes we are forced to do things that we don't normally would. Deadlines can create added pressure.

Do not worry about last-minute tasks and workload

If you're anything like most of us, it happens sometimes at the worst possible times. Last-minute assignments and increased workloads, sickness or emergency, they all come when we least expect them.

These situations could be obstacles to us achieving our goals. You might have to choose whether you are learning or fulfilling other obligations. Sometimes we can't stop doing what we do to help with another obligation.

It is impossible to control everything in this life. We are not able to control how our bosses make us feel or increase our workload. We are not able to control what happens when we become sick or when there are emergencies. We can't predict the future and we can't plan for it.

Proactive learning and a willingness to take on new responsibilities before they are due will allow us to adjust our schedule and devote our time to what is most important. It is much easier to delay something for just a day when the deadline is six month away than when you only have a few more days.

You Have Control

Control is the best way to work. If you can set your own schedule, you will feel more relaxed and more likely to accomplish everything without rushing.

Being in control allows you to plan the whole thing, set deadlines and prepare for possible delays. Being in control is about deciding how you want to deal with the situation and not what someone else wants.

You will not be completely in control. It is not possible. You can't have total control over your life. Some people have more control than the rest. You have the ability to make your own decisions. You have the power to decide who you are.

How to be Pro-Active

Proactivity isn't difficult, but it requires discipline. You need to teach yourself how to act at the right time, not just the easiest. You must get into the mindset that the moment you recognize something is necessary, at least you will start to act on it immediately.

It doesn't mean you have to take on the task immediately, but it is important that you incorporate it into your busy schedule. It's okay to know that it won't be due until six months later, but you don't need start working on it right away. It is important to examine your calendar to see when you can work on it. Make a note of it on your calendar or planner, and then get to work.

Prioritizing

Not all things need to be done immediately. While some things can wait, others may need to be done right away. Learning requires that we prioritize what we do and when.

This means we must ensure that we have the correct materials available at all times. Without the necessary materials to help you learn, it is impossible to start learning about a topic. Do not wait until the last moment to order them. So you can get them when you need 'em, order them now. Books and videos often go out-of-stock. It is a waste of time to wait until stock runs out. You have plenty of time to place the backorder and ship your order if you discover it at least one month in advance. Give yourself time.

Make sure you do the most important first. Start with the most important and then move up. Not all items are important and not all can wait six months. You have to decide what must be done and when.

Making Progress

You should set yourself a goal of making progress along the way. You can make up time if you fall behind but you still have plenty of time. If you have a problem, resolve it. Keep your focus on the task at hand. While you may get sidetracked, you shouldn't give up.

Making a Learning Program

A common error made by most people is to try to learn something and not have a plan. This means that they rush to learn blindly believing that everything will just happen by itself.

This rarely happens. If you do not have a plan in place, you can waste time and resources as well as create many gaps throughout the process. It is possible to save time, and still fully grasp the subject. Take a few moments to make your plan at the beginning.

A plan can be thought of as a comprehensive and detailed account of what you should do. Your learning plan does NOT have to be long and complicated. The plan must contain all the information necessary to organize your efforts. It can be as long as 10 pages, 100 pages, or even a post-it note that hangs above the desk. This means that your plan can be as large as you like or as small you don't.

What should your plan contain? That will depend on what you want to learn, but here's a list of the most common items that can be found in a Learning Plan:

What are we trying?

Even though this may sound simple and obvious, it is possible to have high-level learning to obtain an overall education. Other times we will want to learn the specific things that we need. This is why it is essential to clearly identify what items you need and how to get them.

Why are we learning this?

Understanding why we want to learn something is key. This will allow us to appreciate the benefits and potential rewards of this information. This will help us stay motivated during the learning process.

How do we find this information?

We will often feel the need to learn something at a specific time. This could be to obtain a new job or to learn how to garden.

Whatever the reason may be, knowing how much time we have to learn the material allows us to structure our learning plan better to ensure that we devote the correct amount of time each week in order to finish the process when we need it.

This is How Will We Learn It?

Is this going to be via video, audio, written material or a combination? It is helpful to determine which learning style works best for us, so that we can complete the process within the shortest amount of time.

What Materials Are We able to Use?

This is another obvious question, but you should really do some research on the type of learning materials available. Do you have access to videos? If so, which ones work best for you? The same applies to books. Perhaps books come with accompanying videos to make learning even easier.

You might find it helpful to consult more than one source to gain additional insight or information that the author might not share in their books. The best materials will fit your needs and give you the results that you are looking for.

How much time can we realistically spend each week learning?

Many of us think that we can learn endlessly if we really put our minds into learning. Unfortunately, this approach rarely works. To keep you on track, it's much better to create a reasonable learning period that you can devote each week.

Perhaps you decide to dedicate an hour a day to learning your new materials. This won't cause you any major problems and will allow you live your normal life. You will also be able to learn in a more relaxed and stress-free way.

You shouldn't overestimate the amount of time you can dedicate to learning. It is worse to set unrealistic goals and then lose heart. We should set achievable goals, not look for the fastest learners.

What type of Budget do We Have?

There is usually a limit or budget to how much we can spend on something. Although we may want to attend a class at the local college for instance, it's possible that we do not have the funds or desire to spend the $2,000 cost. We need to make other arrangements to be able to spend the amount that we desire.

Seminars can be more expensive than classes, but they are still cheaper than classes. Video and books are the cheapest options when it comes down to purchased material. Even if you have no budget, the library or magazine articles are available to you. It is likely that your budget will have an impact on you, but even those who don't have the budget can still learn if they really wish.

What Resources (Materials? Equipment? Tools) do we need?

It might be enough to study history, math, and other subjects. However, if your goal is to learn how build a deck, how to use power tools, or how garden, you will likely need to have the tools and supplies necessary to do so.

While you may be able to read all you want about how a saw works or how to prepare soil for your gardening, until you actually do the tasks, you'll never know what you are doing. Additional resources are required to perform physical tasks. You might already have some of these resources but others might be needed to be bought, rented, or borrowed. Budgeting can also be affected by these factors.

What can I do to put into practice what I've learned?

Once you have completed the learning process, what next? Sometimes we don't need any follow-up, but other times, we will need to do something in order to use or apply the knowledge.

Remember the saying "If you don't practice it, you lose"? Make sure your plan allows you to put your new knowledge into practice so that you are able to remember more and become better at the task.

Ok, now you see that our plan on creating a plan was very detailed. It took only a few pages and only a short time to create. The length of your plan and the detail it contains will depend on what you are learning.

You will need to plan more detail and a longer learning curve if you want to master something complicated. It will take 4 years to finish a college degree program. This plan will be more complex than learning how build a deck. There is no single model that will provide the best learning plan. Each plan should reflect both the learner and the subject.

Your plan should allow for you to complete the learning process with minimal stress and meet all your objectives.

Establishing Learning Goals

Once we have created our learning plans, let's make it even more complete by adding some goals. Goals are steps from your learning plan that assign real and measured value to those parts. This allows you to easily and quickly determine if you are on schedule or not.

To add goals to any plan, it is simple to set them. The most popular goals are financial, performance, and time. Your plan should include a step to ensure your plan falls within a given budget. Now you can add tangible and quantifiable goals to that step.

One example is if your plan states that you have a $100 budget for your learning process. Your goal might be to complete the process within a budget of 100 dollars. You could also set "mini-goals," which will help you achieve your goal. To help you achieve your main goal, you might add the following: "Spend $50 or less on textbooks, $30 or lower on a movie, $20 or less on supplies, and $30 or less in video games."

To determine how much time it takes to accomplish each step, you will need to take the steps in your plan and set a time limit that you think you should be able complete them within. Consider, for instance, the step in which you determine what materials you have available. You might write "Identify best learning resources by June1".

If you then look at your plans, and you find yourself in the middle of June, you'll quickly realize that you're behind schedule. If it's May 1st, and you have completed this step, you are ahead. Time goals can give you a snapshot of how you're doing relative to where your goal is.

This can make it more difficult to determine performance goals. Performance measurement can sometimes be subjective. It is difficult to determine a value for a particular goal. Test scores will be used in this example. Let's say your goal is to reach the Dean's list next semester. The Dean's list would be your goal. Aim to finish next semester with at least a 3.0 grade point average." If you're in the middle semester and have a 3.9, that is a good result. If your grade is 2.1 or higher, you can stop partying now and start studying!

Goals can be described as numbers that help you see clearly if you are achieving your objectives. They are just a tool to help you stay on-track and focused.

Goals should be realistic and easily achievable. If your goals are too high, you'll get frustrated and lose motivation. If you set your goals too low you won't be able to reach them in a reasonable amount time.

It is important to be honest about your goals. The goal should reflect what you believe you can accomplish. Make them achievable for yourself and not others. This is your plan. It should contain your goals. Be honest with your self and set honest goals.

Sometimes things can go wrong. You might become sick, have a family crisis or find yourself with another task at work that consumes a lot of your time. These things are possible, and they can make it difficult to achieve a goal.

Once that happens, we should sit down and rest our goals in order to make them again possible. You might change the time frame goals if you find that your original goals are too restrictive. Sometimes, the experience is more difficult than expected. If this happens, we should adjust the goals to help us stay motivated.

We don't have to stop working hard and change our goals. Goals should not have to be modified or extended if we feel lazy or don't want to do something. But, if there are legitimate and valid reasons to adjust a goals, then you should do so.

Goals are just tools that can help you reach your goals. Your choices about how to use them (or if at all) are up to your discretion. You can make your learning plan include goals if you want the best chance for success.

Hire Someone!

Sometimes learning through traditional methods such as books, videos, seminars or classes is not the best way to learn. In other cases, learning something from a well-respected expert is the best way. We can then gain the most valuable knowledge in a short period of time by speaking with our expert.

Books and videos can show you how to do things, but they don't give you any experience. The material may be learned, but you won't get the tips and tricks that only experience offers. While this is most often discussed in relation to performing physical tasks, experts can provide more detailed information about history and other subjects.

Experts in their field have a greater depth of knowledge than others. Although the rest of the population may have some knowledge about a subject, experts know much more. Experts also have a lot of personal knowledge.

A mechanic can tell you little tricks over the years that will help you get the best out of your vehicle.

The same way that craftsmen improve their skills and knowledge over time, so too can we take advantage of this by consulting experts in our field. It's possible to speak with people who know what we're interested in, and they can help by sharing real world knowledge.

From my experiences, there are two types in this world. People who know how things work and people who don't. Not just because someone has passed a test or read a book doesn't mean they are an expert. The well-known experts are those who apply the book knowledge to real world experiences.

I have given many training sessions over the years. The lectures and knowledge are great, but what people really enjoy is the hands on instruction or the sharing of their experiences with others. Students' stories, tips, comments, and experiences from others are just as valuable as the instruction.

You should first verify that the person you are trying to learn something from is a recognized expert in their field. You don't have to believe that they are an expert just because they claim it. Make sure to verify references, qualifications, and licenses, if applicable.

It's important to find people that will help you learn the correct way or give you truthful and reliable information. It is not a good idea to learn wrongly, then "unlearn" the lesson and start over. It's much more beneficial to learn the correct way from the beginning.

We are also interested in those who are open to learning and not afraid to share their knowledge. There are many people out there who can help you with the basics but will keep your advanced skills and knowledge to yourself. We don't want them to be our sources. We are looking to people who will help us improve and share all of our knowledge.

Hyper-Speed Learning

Sometimes, it's just not possible to learn something new in an environment that is calm and relaxed. Sometimes we just need to jump in and grab some quick knowledge until we have enough time to learn more. You can use these situations to learn faster and quickly grab the necessary short-term-knowledge.

Before we get to that, I want you to be clear. This should not be your preferred method of learning to speed up and avoid the hard way out. It is possible to learn quickly and efficiently, but it won't likely lead to long-term success. If time is not an issue, you can still benefit from the proven learning strategies and processes in this book.

Here are some tips for those who don't have enough time.

Get someone to prove it

If you're trying to learn something visually like how to repair or rebuild something, then you should find someone with the necessary knowledge and experience and ask them to demonstrate it to you.

It is just the ability of seeing something happening right in front of your eyes and being able to see it in three dimensions, using all of your senses instead of looking at a screen or monitor can give you lots of information quickly. It can also help to save time and allow you to ask questions.

Take someone along to work

Sometimes it's a good idea even if your knowledge is limited to working alongside someone who has experience with the subject. Perhaps you should talk to someone with more in-depth knowledge about a topic so you can clarify your doubts, get more details and answer any questions.

Take a look at this video

Nowadays, it's easier than ever to access a large number of instructional videos and other information. A video can help you with anything from hobbies to construction to repair to any physical task.

I actually check the videos on everything before I do it for the first time. This is especially important when you are working on different versions of the same thing. Watching the video can help you save time, as it shows where certain things are located and how to work on them.

YouTube is a great place to find videos. You can watch a five minute video in a matter of minutes and get valuable information along the way.

Please read the Summary or the Introduction.

Sometimes a summary or introductory version of a subject is available. This allows you to learn the main points and not get into detail. Even though this may not provide the depth of information you need to understand the topic fully, it can give you a good overview of the key points.

If you find yourself in a situation when you need to talk with someone about something that is not your specialty, this can be very helpful. You can quickly pick up the basics and begin to understand enough to be able at least to communicate intelligently with someone about it.

Sometimes books and videos will include a quick start section. This gives you an overview before you dive into the deeper material. While this might help you get to the main points of the book, it is not enough. Don't try to cover more than you can handle.

Pick & Choose

Many times, we just want to master a particular aspect of a bigger issue. However, we don't necessarily need to know the whole thing. One example: I might want to learn how repair my own vehicle but, for now, I just need to change the engine.

I then purchase a manual on auto repairs and simply go to the chapter about oil changes to learn how to change my oil. I can later go back to the guide and read more about changing air filters, bleeding brakes, or other procedures. For now, all I want is to change my engine oil.

Remember that there are times when other skills are required to complete a task or learn the basics. You need to be aware and to make sure you read those sections. You may be able to skip to the section you need and just read the material. It's still much faster than starting on page one and reading through the entire book.

Hire Someone to Assist or Observe

We had discussed working with someone. This idea takes that one step further.

Perhaps you should hire someone to teach you something about a current situation. You may even be able assist with the process.

The benefits of hiring an expert are many that you might not have realized. It allows you to access immediate expertise whenever you require it. Second, you can see the process firsthand so you can decide if your abilities and capabilities will allow you to handle this type of task in the future. While we might have great intentions, everyone isn't able to handle every task. This is why you can find people who are able to help with just about everything.

If hiring someone is an option, make sure you are able to find someone who is skilled and has a few recommendations. This is far better than picking from the random yellow pages.

Do it!

Sometimes, it's enough to ignore all warnings and just do the job. It is important to realize that we are not likely to fail if this happens. If this is the case, we may have to face the music and miss the deadline or accept our fate.

However, if there is a minor or major downside, we might want to just do our best, apply common sense, and get on with the job. It is possible to buy a book on the subject, and then open it and refer to it as needed throughout the entire process. Even though this will take longer to complete, it's still possible.

If I need a graphic design for a particular project, I might not be familiar with the graphics program. Normally, the graphics department or our graphic person handles this for me. But she is either sick or on vacation. There are two options. You can either go ahead, pull out the manual or try to do it yourself.

There will be many situations when we are required to learn something new. However, if you use common sense, have the right learning materials and are organized, you can learn anything.

Our results at first may be crude and less professional. However, in times of crisis, drastic measures are often required. It is good to experience firsthand the fact that we can accomplish what we need even when we're not fully prepared.